Original title:
Across the Event Horizon

Copyright © 2025 Creative Arts Management OÜ
All rights reserved.

Author: Colin Harrington
ISBN HARDBACK: 978-1-80567-831-1
ISBN PAPERBACK: 978-1-80567-952-3

Whispers of the Singularity

In a realm where time goes slow,
The clocks have all lost their flow.
Einstein's laughing in his chair,
Saying, 'You might want to beware!'

Gravity's pulling your socks down,
Spinning like a topsy clown.
Matter dances in whirly twirls,
While sing-along shadows give twirls.

Dance of Dark Matter

In the dark, it likes to pratfall,
Bumping into everything, what a ball!
Invisible friends with silly jokes,
Wobbling around like clumsy folks.

It hides when you try to confront,
Regular matter just can't front.
Trading secrets, it loves to cheer,
Play hide and seek with cosmic beer.

Symphony of Shadows and Light

The shadows play a jazzy beat,
While the light skips on tiny feet.
Together they frolic in the void,
Making the universe feel overjoyed.

Sunbeams and gloom have a grand ball,
They've invited all, big and small.
The notes echo in a cosmic splash,
Creating a melody that's quite the clash!

Voyage to the Edge of Perception

Pack your bags, we're off to play,
To a place where things seem gray.
Where perceptions twist around and jive,
And only the oddest thoughts can survive.

The view's a riddle, quite absurd,
Where nothing is said, but all is heard.
Hold tight, we're steering through the haze,
On a whimsical quest, a curious maze!

The Call of the Infinite Night

In a universe feels quite absurd,
Stars wear glasses, have you heard?
Galaxies giggle, spinning around,
While comets make a whooshing sound.

Black holes play peek-a-boo game,
Sucking light, but never the same.
Astronauts dance like they're in a dream,
Floating like jelly, or so it would seem.

Planets in costumes, what a delight,
Venus wore polka-dots, oh what a sight!
Mars brought the snacks, an interstellar treat,
While Saturn's rings gave the party some beat.

In this cosmic circus, laughter resounds,
Even dark matter's spinning around.
So join the party in the night sky,
With aliens laughing, oh me, oh my!

Rifts in the Fabric of Time

The clock just went and lost its mind,
Tick-tock dance, a groove so blind.
Seconds tumble, laughter flows,
Is it tea time or just my toes?

Pants that vanish, shoes that fly,
Dear old cat has learned to sigh.
Dimensions bend and twist about,
I just found my lunch, no doubt!

When Light Meets the Dark

A beam of light in cozy gloom,
Said, "Why don't we check the room?"
The shadows giggled, played a game,
Whispered secrets without shame.

A dance-off, bright and bold,
But dark kept stepping on its hold.
"You shine so bright, but can you groove?"
Light replied, "Let's make a move!"

The Gravity of Lost Dreams

Oh, dreams that fell, so heavy, dear,
Caught in a black hole, round and clear.
I swear I lost my socks in there,
Along with hope and my last hair.

Prepare the launch, it's time for flight,
Get shoelaces tied and spirits bright.
When dreams get stuck, just wiggle and spin,
For even black holes know how to grin!

Echoes from the Void

In the silence, a voice did shout,
"Is anybody home?" - no one about.
A echo replied with a comical tone,
"Just me and my thoughts, please don't moan!"

The void was fun, a cosmic party,
Where lost balloons danced, oh so hearty.
With giggles galore and stars on spree,
In the dark, we found the silliest glee!

Where Time Stops and Starts

In a place where clocks go slow,
Past the point of what we know.
Flipping pancakes in zero G,
Wondering if I'm lost at sea.

Jellybeans float, and so do we,
Tea parties held on a cosmic spree.
With gravity on a coffee break,
We dance on stars, make no mistake!

The Veil Between Worlds

Behind the curtain of the night,
A game of hide and seek with light.
Ghosts with laugh tracks make us grin,
Whispering secrets, their silly kin.

Do you think that they can cook?
What's on the menu? Let's take a look!
Boo! A joke from the spectral crew,
In this spooky café, sit down for two!

Celestial Reflections

Mirrors hang in the void so black,
Each one holds a cosmic snack.
Popcorn stars and nebula sauce,
Eating stardust, oh what a loss!

Chasing shadows with moonbeam rays,
Laughter echoes in spacey ways.
Just don't bump into a comet's tail,
Or you might find yourself on a whale!

The Pull of the Unknown

In the grip of a wobbly fate,
I'm pulled by the weird, can't hesitate.
Banana peels on asteroid trails,
Floating on jokes and giggling gales.

With each twist, a new dance step,
I've got my spacesuit, feeling prepped.
Bad puns galore as we twist and twirl,
In the unknown, let laughter unfurl!

The Hidden Currents of Time

In a dance where the clocks just spin,
The past trips over its own chin.
Time's wearing socks on its hands,
While we're all lost in shifting sands.

Wormholes play peek-a-boo with fate,
"Are we late?" they say, "No, just great!"
The seconds waltz with much delight,
As we chase shadows into the night.

The Last Light of Distant Worlds

A star went out for a coffee break,
Left the universe in a big mistake.
It said, "I'll be back in a light year or two!"
But now we're here wondering what to do.

Planets zoom by on their cosmic quest,
In sneakers of gravity, they're kind of a pest.
"Hey Earth, catch up!" they call in disdain,
While we scratch our heads, "Is that a comet or plane?"

Horizons of Uncertainty

A spaceship showed up; it's a fancy one,
With blinking lights that promise fun.
But nobody knows how to drive it, oh dear,
As we all scream, "Just grab the gear!"

Out there in space, it gets really weird,
With aliens saying, "We've all sneered!"
They laugh and hover, eating our snacks,
While we're stuck here, unsure of our tracks.

Sirens of the Celestial Deep

The sirens sing in a galactic choir,
But their tune sounds more like a tire.
"Dance with us, mortals, it's all in good fun!"
As they twirl through stars and a glowing bun.

With stars in their hair and laughter so bright,
They paint the cosmos with colors of light.
Yet we keep tripping over our own feet,
Saying, "Don't pull me in; I'm really quite sweet!"

The Infinite Unknown Beckons

The cosmos calls with a silly grin,
Where gravity dances and quirks begin.
Stars wear hats, comets all chase,
A universe full of laughable space.

Planets in pajamas, what a sight!
Orbiting suns with their party lights.
Asteroids break-dancing, oh, what a show,
Who knew the void could put on a glow?

Black holes giggle, pulling you in,
What's left of your snacks? Not even a tin!
So grab your telescope, bring some cheer,
The infinite unknown is finally here!

With every twinkling star that we see,
We're riding the waves of cosmic glee.
So come take a trip, it's a wild ride,
In this wacky universe, come join the tide!

Secrets Hidden in the Starlight.

Whispers of laughter in the cosmic sea,
Stars share secrets as bright as can be.
Aliens gossip about Earthlings' trends,
Did you see what they wore? Oh, that never ends!

Nebulas blossom, like cotton candy clouds,
While planets look sassy, wearing space shrouds.
Galaxies twirl in a cosmic ballet,
Making time wobble; oh, what a display!

Astrophysics jokes that fly past our heads,
Like comets with wigs and interstellar beds.
Einstein's quirks dance in rings quite absurd,
Amongst the stardust, life's blissfully blurred.

So peer into the sky, take a hearty laugh,
For hidden delights are the universe's half.
In the twinkle of starlight, we chuckle and play,
Secrets are waiting, come out and sway!

Into the Abyssal Unknown

Diving deep into the silly void,
Where logic's a plaything, and facts are toyed.
Space is a carnival, laughter our thread,
With wobbly quarks doing the cha-cha instead!

Black holes are like whirlpools of mirth,
Swallowing thoughts; oh, what a birth!
A dance with the cosmos, a waltz with the stars,
Where the punchline is always behind Mars.

Aliens in costumes, oh, what a sight!
Throwing intergalactic parties at night.
With popcorn made of stardust and fun,
Who knew the abyss could be such a pun?

So into the unknown, let's plunge and dive,
A whimsical voyage, come feel alive!
In laughter, we drift through space's delight,
Finding joy in the shadows of endless night!

Beyond the Cosmic Veil

Behind the curtain of the night sky,
Giggles and wiggles swirl and fly.
Asteroids chuckle as they roll on by,
In this playful cosmos, we laugh and sigh.

Constellations gossip and tell silly tales,
While meteors swoosh with their rainbow trails.
The universe winks, with a glimmer of fun,
Each star twinkling, saying, 'Join the run!'

The void is not empty, it's jolly and bright,
Where starlight's a dance floor, and we're all in sight.
With cosmic confetti and laughter that swells,
Beyond the veil, we break all the spells.

So let's float on laughter, on stardust we thrive,
In this whimsical cosmos, it's fun being alive!
With jokes bouncing off the celestial walls,
Join the laughter, as the universe calls!

Fragments of Light in the Dark

In a cosmos so vast, I lost my shoe,
A star twinkled down, said, "Try a new view!"
Space dust tickled my nose and my toes,
I laughed as I floated, where nobody goes.

A comet zoomed by, wanted a race,
"You can't catch me!" I yelled, feeling out of place.
With planets for friends, we danced in the night,
Spinning around like we just took flight.

My flashlight flickered, oh what a sight,
Guiding lost aliens, so full of delight.
They tripped on their antennae, what a clatter!
Who knew light-years could end in such banter?

In voids where the funny makes waiting worthwhile,
I found spicy stardust that made me smile.
With each silly twirl, a giggle took flight,
In cosmic confusion, all felt just right.

The Beyond Where Stars Whisper

In a sky that giggles and whispers at me,
Stars are just marbles, floating carefree.
I tossed one to my friend, who caught it with glee,
"Now we own a planet, let's drink some tea!"

Planets tried to chat, but it sounded like hums,
"Sorry, I'm not fluent in your awkward drums!"
I sipped my space juice, it tasted bizarre,
Thought I'd find a burger, but found just a star.

A black hole tripped me, oh what a thud,
"Watch your step!" it chuckled, "You're lost in the mud!"
I laughed as I spun in its merry old dance,
Hoping the end of the line held a chance.

Quasars cracked jokes while I floated about,
Each punchline a comet, I howled with a shout.
In the laughs of the cosmos, I found my sweet place,
The universe tickled my funny bone's space.

Navigating the Dark Tides

Sailing on starlight, I took the wrong turn,
Found myself flipping, oh what a concern!
A wave of dark laughter crashed over my head,
Turns out the ocean is just cosmic bread.

I tried to surf moons, which acted so coy,
"No, thank you, good Earthling, we prefer a toy!"
So I built a sandcastle, made out of stars,
But it melted away—thanks to some Mars cars.

Galactic jellyfish floated past with style,
They whispered sweet nothings that made me smile.
I waved back politely, but one gave me fright,
Tangled in lights, what a comical sight!

With every wave's crash, I learned how to glide,
Navigating laughter through this cosmic tide.
No map, just the joy, my compass a grin,
In the silly unknown, let adventures begin!

Horizons Beyond the Known

What lies beyond where the map says 'beware,'
A dance of odd wonders in music and air.
I stumbled upon a parade of lost socks,
They jiggled and wiggled, ignoring all clocks.

The moons wore top hats, the stars donned a dress,
It seemed so absurd, but I had to confess.
A nebula grand was singing a tune,
While space made a joke that made crickets swoon.

I tried to fit in, but my shoes were too tight,
As comets cracked jokes that soared through the night.
"Join us, dear friend, we're the laugh riot crew!"
In a universe spinning, we lightened the blue.

So if you feel stranded in cosmic embrace,
Just look for the laughter; it sets the right pace.
For in every dark corner, there's humor to find,
A giggle, a chuckle, the universe's kind.

Whispers of the Singularity

In a realm where time plays tricks,
I lost my socks, can't find the mix.
Black holes giggle and stars poke fun,
While I dance with gravity, just begun.

The universe laughs, it sways and spins,
Twirling in chaos, where no one wins.
I tried to waltz with a neutron star,
But it laughed too hard, flung me too far.

Quasars sing with a comical tone,
While cosmic dust makes my hair overgrown.
I asked a comet for stellar advice,
It told me to party, and roll the dice.

So here I am, a cosmic clown,
Floating along in a sparkly gown.
With every twist and turn I make,
The universe chuckles, for goodness' sake!

Dance of Light and Shadow

In the ballroom of space, the shadows twirl,
Light zips around in an energetic whirl.
I stepped on a photon, it laughed with glee,
"Careful there, buddy, don't step on me!"

The blackness winks, a mischievous tease,
While stars do the cha-cha just to please.
I tried to lead a dance with a quasar,
But it spun me around, flung me too far.

Gravity's tune, a wobbly beat,
Wobbling along, I stumbled on my feet.
The moon pulled a prank, hid behind a cloud,
And I twirled in circles, feeling quite proud.

With each lunar step, my feet grew light,
Dancing through the cosmos, day and night.
In this silly ballet, I find my bliss,
As starlight and shadows swirl and kiss.

Secrets of the Gravitational Abyss

Down into the depths where the tickles reside,
Ghosts of lost planets in gravitational glide.
I asked a black hole if I could fit,
It chuckled and said, "Let's see if you're it!"

I tossed in my lunch, saw it disappear,
The void giggled, saying, "No fear!"
I tried to outrun a runaway star,
It laughed too hard; I never got far.

Whispers of secrets in space's embrace,
Wormholes wink at me, a comical race.
I slipped on a comet, it sent me shouldering,
Right past the planets, cartwheeling, tumbling.

What treasures await in this cosmic abyss?
Jokes about gravity, can't help but reminisce.
With each twist and turn, I proudly insist,
The universe loves a good laugh, I insist!

The Lure of the Cosmic Abyss

Out in the darkness, where stars have a bash,
The cosmic abyss holds wonders to clash.
I followed a pulsar, thought it'd be cool,
Ended up in a nebula – what's the rule?

Had a date with a quasar, or so it seemed,
But it opened its mouth, and I nearly screamed.
The light years flew by, took a bit of time,
As I fumbled and stumbled – cosmic slapstick prime.

I chased after meteors, thought I could catch,
They giggled and zigged, like darts in a match.
A meteorite winked, said, "Play with glee!"
But I tripped and fell, on cosmic debris.

Yet still, there's a charm in this endless chase,
A dance with the void, a humorous grace.
Though the stars may play tricks with their glowing kisses,
I find joy in the laughter – the best of wishes!

Chasing the Light's Last Breath

When the sun began to yawn,
I tripped on cosmic dust,
A race with photons bright,
I spilled my stardust drink.

My shadow laughed and danced,
As I chased a twinkling star,
It winked and zipped away,
I guess it's just too far.

What's faster than a thought?
A squirrel in a rocket suit!
Zooming past the galaxies,
With him I must commute.

When I fell into a void,
I found a comfy chair,
With snacks of space and time,
I rocked without a care.

Secrets Beneath the Starlit Sea

Under waves of twinkling lights,
I found a fish with shoes,
"Why do you march in silence?"
He winked and said, "It's news!"

The octopus wore glasses,
Studying the cosmic pies,
He said the universe is sweet,
With flavors that surprise.

A dolphin sang of journeys,
Beyond the tides and swells,
He said he heard a secret,
In echoes, not in bells.

So we danced beneath the stars,
With laughter haunting night,
A splash of cosmic wonder,
Made everything feel bright.

The Dimensional Drift

I hopped from one place to the next,
Through wormholes, I would leap,
In one land, I was a king,
In the next, just a sheep.

My spaceship looked like broccoli,
It smelled like old wet socks,
But it flew with such great gusto,
Dodging all the blocks.

I met a cat that spoke in rhyme,
And danced upon the air,
He said, "For fun, let's drift away,
To places full of flair!"

So we twirled through time and space,
With giggles filling voids,
A goofy sort of chaos,
In realms where joy's employed.

Journey to the Uncharted Realm

We packed our bags for journeys wide,
With snacks from every store,
Our map was drawn by chance and tides,
"Let's explore!" we swore.

The ship was made of waffle cones,
With sails of cotton candy,
"Don't eat the sides," I warned my friends,
"Or we'll be left as dandy!"

We tripped on skies of purple goo,
And slid through cosmic rain,
Where jellybeans grew on trees,
And chocolate ruled the plain.

With hiccups we would tumble,
Through realms of silly dreams,
This journey was quite bumpy,
But oh, how fun it seems!

The Unseen Frontier

In a vacuum, there's no sound,
Yet my cat thinks she's profound.
She pounces on dust, makes a scene,
Staring at shadows, quite the queen.

Wormholes wobble like silly jigs,
As I chase after cosmic pigs.
They swirl and twirl in gravity's dance,
But really, they just want a chance.

Aliens may not like our jokes,
They laugh at our sunshine and smoke.
They sent a meme, it's quite the fright,
Of cats floating in the moonlight.

A rocket's launch, a fateful aim,
Yet here I am, forgetting my name.
As I zip through space, oh what a thrill,
I trip on my tongue, what a skill!

Transcending the Celestial Boundary

Stars wear hats made of pure light,
They dance around, quite the sight.
I asked them for a cosmic tour,
But they just laughed and wanted more.

Comets with tails like a cat's swish,
Bump into planets, make a wish.
"Oops, my bad!" the comet cries,
As Jupiter rolls its merry eyes.

A galaxy hiccups, spills some gas,
Planets wobble, "Hey! Watch your class!"
Black holes giggle, swirling around,
As I trip over time, quite unbound.

Asteroids tossing like a ball,
Who knew space could be such a brawl?
As I float along, enjoying the ride,
The universe grins; there's nowhere to hide!

Embrace of the Infinite Night

In the dark, where shadows play,
The moon gives a wink, 'What do you say?'
Stars giggle loud in their crystal capes,
Creating some plans, bypassing shapes.

A dance-off starts between bright suns,
Gravity's got moves with no runs.
They twirl and spin, it's quite a blast,
But blue giants fell, they can't outlast.

Galaxies whisper all their tales,
Of cosmic winds and shipwrecked sails.
Distant worlds giggle at my plight,
As I reach for snacks in the cosmic night.

So here I float, on ice cream dreams,
With rocket popsicles and moonbeam gleams.
Nothing's too strange, in this starry plight,
Just a cosmic giggle in the infinite night!

Beyond the Threshold of Stars

Through the doorway made of stardust,
I stumble back, my pants all rust.
A cosmos of jellybeans in sight,
I wonder if aliens share my bite!

Galactic creatures, freaky and fun,
They bring me snacks and a laser gun.
"Take aim at the Quasar!" they yell with glee,
But we miss and hit the cat on a spree.

Time travels like a rollercoaster ride,
Down the Milky Way, I glide and slide.
With each twist, I'm met with a grin,
As squirrels in space throw nuts like a win!

So here I am, a traveler bold,
In space's embrace, oh, what a hold.
With laughter echoing through the bizarre,
I dance with the comets, my cosmic star!

Singularity's Call

In a cosmic swirl, I lost my shoe,
Fell through a portal, oh what a view!
Dancing with quarks, I'm feeling bold,
Chasing a star that's slightly too cold.

My coffee floats, defying all laws,
A space-time dance, with temporal flaws.
Gravity chuckles as I drift and sway,
Wishing a comet would take me away.

In black hole depths, I spotted a cat,
He winked and said, "You can't sit like that!"
With every spin, I'm closer to glee,
A singular joke on the cosmos and me.

Celestial Anomalies Unveiled

Twinkling lights in the sky, what a tease,
Told me to check if my brain's at ease.
UFOs zoom past, saying, "What's your deal?"
I replied, "I'm just here for a cosmic meal!"

In interstellar bars, they serve moon cheese,
With side orders of starlight, if you please.
Chasing shooting stars, I trip and fall,
Bumping my head on the cosmic wall.

Black holes laugh as I try to flee,
What's the rush in this vast, endless spree?
I'll trade a comet for a side of fries,
While Martians groove to my silly cries.

The Pull of the Unknown

I feel the tug of those strange celestial waves,
Like a cosmic dance party in the light of caves.
I packed my bags, with snacks in tow,
For a trip through a vortex, my face aglow.

With every step, I hear a space tune,
Jupiter's got a band, jamming at noon.
I waved to the asteroids, beckoning me,
"Come join our ride, it's wild and free!"

Planets spin lazily, I join in the race,
Tripping on stardust, what a funny place!
As stars start winking, the giggles ignite,
In a universe where everything feels light.

Dreams Beneath the Cosmic Veil

Drifting through dreams made of stardust beams,
Laughed with a nebula bursting with schemes.
It whispered of futures, oh so bizarre,
I texted my dog, "I'm a space rock star!"

Floating in cosmos, I saw a bright sign,
"Free space hugs!" I said, "Sounds divine!"
Eagerly I looped through a loop-de-loop,
It's hard to feel serious when you're in a scoop!

With comets making faces, I started to cheer,
Saying, "To infinity, let's grab a beer!"
And so we laughed 'neath the shimmer and veil,
Cosmic antics never grow stale.

The Liminal Space of Stars

In a place where socks lose pairs,
Galaxies giggle with cosmic flares.
Where time takes a nap under a quirky tree,
And space bends over laughing at you and me.

Gravity's a joke, it's not what it seems,
Tripping on stardust and whimsical dreams.
A wobbly dance on a comet's bright tail,
We'll sip on blue milk and ride the comet's trail.

Quasars play peek-a-boo with black holes,
While celestial beings play bingo with souls.
Floating around in this funny old night,
We'll trade our best jokes for total starlight.

So let's skip and frolic through nebulae bright,
With space as our playground, everything feels right.
Let laughter and joy be our guiding star,
In this liminal place, we'll never go far.

The Color of Nothingness

What's the hue of a black hole's frown?
Or the shade of a star when it tumbles down?
Is it bubblegum pink or mustardy green?
When voids decide to throw a color bean?

Perhaps it's a blend, a swirl of the bizarre,
Like cosmic cotton candy from a space bazaar.
A splash of laughter, a dash of despair,
Drawing doodles with photons, light as a chair.

We paint nothingness with brushes of fun,
While aliens giggle in the shade of the sun.
With a wink and a nod, they plot their great scheme,
To color the cosmos with a vibrant meme.

So cheer up the gaps, where nothing does dwell,
Add a glittery gleam or a playful yell.
In this awesome void, we'll craft our parade,
Coloring nothingness, our grand escapade.

When Dreams Touch the Void

In a dreamlit world where wishes collide,
With a giggle and twirl, let's go for a ride.
We'll tickle the clouds and skate on the stars,
While whispers of nothingness echo from Mars.

With wishes like bubbles that float through the night,
And dreams that bounce high, oh what a sight!
In this playful dance, we'll dodge black holes,
While trading our stories and funny old scrolls.

When shadows dance lightly and laughter abounds,
We'll turn voids into playgrounds, no limits, just sounds.
With beams of delight, we'll reach for the sky,
As dreams touch the void and laughter goes high.

So let's soar through the darkness, fearless and bright,
With a wink and a grin, taking off into night.
In the realm of the dreamers, where giggles ignite,
Each touch of the void reminds us: it's light.

Under the Cosmic Canopy

Beneath a sky draped in glitter and glee,
We lounge with the stars for a cosmic tea.
Planets play hopscotch, and comets eat pie,
While meteors swoosh with a funny goodbye.

Under the tent of the cosmos so vast,
We roast marshmallows while time flies past.
With gravity's pull on a trampoline floor,
We bounce and we giggle, who could ask for more?

As the universe grins, we dance with delight,
Trading our tails with each twinkling light.
For laughter's the language, and joy's our refrain,
In this cosmic canopy, we'll always remain.

So gather the stars and let's make our toast,
To the wonders of space that inspire the most.
Under this blanket, so soft and so wide,
We'll giggle and play, with the cosmos our guide.

Where Time Bends and Space Collides

In a world where clocks run amok,
Time slips and slides, like a duck on a rock.
Gravity pulls, like a toddler's hug,
We laugh as we drift, no need for a plug.

Pies fly by in this cosmic ballet,
Eating dessert? Oh, there's always a delay!
Scientists search for that one little clue,
While we sip on tea, watching space cows moo.

Planets do pirouettes on invisible strings,
Aliens dance to the tune that life brings.
We wear our best hats, in this merry affair,
As the universe chuckles, beyond all compare.

So hold on your dreams, let them take flight,
In this zany realm, everything feels right.
With every big bang and each wormhole twist,
We find that the absurd is hard to resist.

Shadows in the Starlit Abyss

In the dark, where shadows play tricks,
Laughter echoes loud, just like silly flicks.
Stars are our lanterns, shining so bright,
Making shadows dance with all of their might.

Jupiter's grinning, with moons all around,
While Saturn's rings play hopscotch on the ground.
Comets zoom past, dripping space goo,
As we giggle and chuckle, it's quite a zoo!

Black holes are shy, hiding from the light,
But space monsters rave, what a goofy sight!
We tease the cosmos, the jokes on the stars,
As we twirl through the void, in our jammy cars.

So here's to the shadows that move with flair,
In this cosmic night, we're free as the air.
With every silly thought, our spirits do rise,
In the starlit abyss, we dance to the skies.

Echoes from the Blackened Depths

In the blackened depths where darkness does sing,
Echoes of laughter, oh what joy they bring!
Whispers of comets, tales of space laws,
Even the black holes snicker and pause.

We surf on stardust, riding the wave,
Singing to quasars, oh how we crave!
Galaxies giggle, spinning 'round tight,
Caught in this cosmic, bewildering light.

Don't mind the gravity, it's just a phase,
In this wacky universe, we play for days.
If we trip on a quark, just laugh and get up,
Pour some tea in a nebula, fill up your cup!

So raise a toast to laughter in space,
A journey of joy in this vast, silly place.
With echoes that bounce, from depth to the sky,
We'll dance with the stars until the day we die.

The Gravity of Silence

In silence, we float, like dust on the breeze,
Where whispers of starlight bring us to our knees.
Gravity giggles, pulling us near,
While we share silly jokes, drinking cosmic beer.

Black holes are shy, hiding their faces,
In this calm of the void, we find funny places.
Silent are the laughs of worlds gone by,
Yet here in our bubble, we soar and we fly.

As meteors tumble, we burst into glee,
Counting the stars, just you and me.
Space might be quiet, but our hearts are loud,
Lost in our laughter, feeling so proud.

So let's float through the cosmos, hand in hand,
With the silence around us, it's perfectly planned.
For in every still moment, a giggle will rise,
In the gravity of silence, we dance with the skies.

The Twilight Between Dimensions

In the middle of a cosmic jest,
Aliens ponder, who's the best?
Time does backflips, space walks a line,
Where marshmallows float while stars sip wine.

A cat wearing glasses reads the news,
In a universe filled with quirky views.
The clocks twist around like a ribbon of fate,
While popcorn pops at a galactic rate.

Planets are disco balls spinning bright,
Asteroids dance in the soft starlight.
Gravity chuckles, pulls us close yet apart,
In a waltz that makes even black holes smart.

With laughter echoing through the vast, dark void,
We find cosmic quirks we can't avoid.
So, join the party, don't miss the spree,
In this twilight zone where strange is glee.

The Secret Song of Black Holes

A black hole hums a secret tune,
With quarks and leptons dancing soon.
It swallows laughter, whole worlds tight,
While spacetime jiggles, oh what a sight!

Inside, a voodoo choir sings so sweet,
While lost socks form a cosmic beat.
The event horizon rolls its eyes,
As wobbly planets wear silly ties.

Galactic hiccups make stars erupt,
In this interstellar tea party, we're all corrupt!
What goes in may never come back out,
But that won't stop us from laughing, no doubt.

So tune your ears to that slurping sound,
In the realm of the lost, joy can be found.
With each giggle, a new star is born,
In this symphony of chaos, we blissfully adorn.

Beyond the Gravitational Dance

In the waltz of gravity's gentle sigh,
The planets quirk and giggle, oh my!
Saturn wears rings like a fancy hat,
While comets race by, yelling "Look at that!"

Asteroids trip in a cosmic conga,
While stars play tag and grow a bit fonder.
Neptune's feeling a little too blue,
So it starts to prank its old pal, too.

Black holes spin tales of what's lost and found,
As space-time tickles the edges around.
In this dance of mirth where galaxies twirl,
Even the vacuum gives a soft swirl.

With each pirouette, we laugh and sway,
In the universe's quirky cabaret.
So grab your partner, glide with the stars,
In this gravitational party, we're all avatars.

Embracing the Unknowable

Out in the cosmos, we ponder with glee,
What if the dark just wants to be free?
Objects unfurl in a wink of the eye,
While quarks tease electrons, saying goodbye.

The unknown tickles like a featherbed,
As theories bounce 'round inside our head.
Schrodinger's cat holds a party in space,
With one foot in here and the other a race.

Philosophers chuckle, trying to reflect,
On physics that bends, twists, and connects.
The cosmos whispers, "Don't take it too serious,
In the game of the stars, life's truly delirious!"

So embrace the mysteries, dance in the dark,
With a wink from a quasar, we'll leave our mark.
In the grand scheme of things, let laughter decree,
That the unknown is just a curious spree!

Dreaming Beyond the Cosmic Curtain

In a spaceship made of cheese,
We zoomed past stars with such ease.
The aliens waved, their hands all frayed,
As we blasted off with our cosmic charade.

Floating by with bubble gum,
We laughed at planets feeling glum.
With a flick of a wand, we twirled in delight,
Making comets dance through the endless night.

Asteroids tossed like birthday cake,
Each one a wish we'd surely make.
We'd trade them for a funky hat,
And ride a wave on a friendly cat.

So here we spin in our silly quest,
In the universe, we jest the best.
With every giggle, we stretch and yawn,
In a cosmic show that goes on and on.

Trails of the Fading Light

Starlight flickers, a game of tag,
We chased it down in a cosmic rag.
With a leap and a skip through the darkened glow,
We giggled at how the shadows flow.

Planets twirl like dancers in shoes,
Spinning round while we share our snooze.
A waltz with space in pajamas bright,
We moonwalk across the velvet night.

No guidebooks here for this wild ride,
Just a map made of dreams and a playful slide.
We bounced on beams of fading light,
A celestial game, oh what a sight!

So when the stars begin to fade,
We'll laugh and cheer for the fun we made.
In the trails of light, we find delight,
As we zip through the cosmos, a joyful sight.

Unraveling the Cosmic Tapestry

Weaving stars with yarn so bright,
Creating patterns in the night.
With every stitch, a laugh or two,
As we crafted worlds, just me and you.

Galaxies spin in a spiral dance,
While we giggle at their clumsy prance.
Every thread has a funny tale,
Of space socks lost in a cosmic gale.

Nebulae bloom like flowers in spring,
While we joke about the joys they bring.
A universe made from silly dreams,
Knitted together in playful seams.

So let's unspool this grand old weave,
Adding color to all who believe.
In this tapestry of cosmic cheer,
We find the funny things we hold dear.

The Weight of the Void

Floating freely in empty space,
We giggle at a lack of a race.
With no one here to call us out,
We dance and twirl, without a doubt.

Weights of nothing, oh what fun,
We juggled black holes and laughed on the run.
With silly faces, we tried to pout,
But the void kept chuckling, round about.

In this endless silence, we became lights,
Bouncing jokes off meteoric heights.
Gravity? Nah! It took the day off,
We floated by and let out a scoff.

So here in nothing, we find our glee,
Making the universe a comedy spree.
The weight of the void? Just a jest,
As we embrace this cosmic fest!

Gazing into the Infinite

Looking up at the night sky,
Stars winking like they're shy.
I asked a comet, 'Hey, how's it going?'
It zoomed away — no signs of knowing.

Planets swirl like a cosmic dance,
Twirling round in a stellar trance.
I tried to wave, but they just spun,
Guess interstellar friends are fun!

Black holes yawn like they're bored,
Sucking in all, they can't be stored.
I dropped my snack, it disappeared,
That's how lunch plans are often cleared!

Galaxies giggle, they spin so fast,
Chasing each other, making a blast.
If aliens see this, what will they think?
'We need more popcorn, grab a drink!'

The Edge of Forever

At the brink of time, I took a peek,
Saw an old dog — it looked so chic!
He barked at me with a cosmic grin,
Then jumped into the void — let the fun begin!

Time travelers bustled, dressed in style,
One lost his hat; he ran a mile.
I offered him an ice cream cone,
But he time-jumped, now I'm alone.

Rockets zoom past with a loud whoosh,
I waved one down — it sped like a gushing sush.
The pilot yelled, 'Get on or you're late!'
Too bad I tripped; I missed the fate!

With every tick, the universe giggles,
In the space-time stream, reality wiggles.
'Forever is just a long coffee break,'
They chuckled, then vanished — what a mistake!

Between the Stars and the Unknown

Floating in space, I lost my shoe,
Poking a nebula, it turned blue!
'Excuse me,' I said, 'now where's my foot?'
It chuckled back, 'You're quite a hoot!'

In a void where no one speaks,
I spotted a squid with cosmic beaks.
It announced, 'Let's dance, it's quite the groove!'
We did the worm, and I found my move!

Passing ships exchanged goofy grins,
Space jokes fly — just look at their fins!
One said, 'Why did the comet break up?'
'It needed more space, that's what's up!'

Drifting good vibes and galactic cheer,
Life in the stars is quite sincere.
With every laugh, we float and spin,
Just looking for fun, where to begin?

Silence of the Celestial Abyss

In the dark where echoes play,
I tripped on stardust — what a buffet!
Bumping into shadows without a sound,
Lost in giggles that swirl around.

Asteroids rolling like marbles in the night,
I chased one down — it took flight!
Waving to aliens munching on fries,
They tossed me a burger — what a surprise!

In the quiet of dark matter's embrace,
I burst into laughter, oh what a race!
With each cosmic giggle, I twirled,
Making silly faces, my joy unfurled.

As I danced in the dark of the void,
Worries vanished, troubles destroyed.
Laughter rings out, the universe grins,
In the silence, my cosmic fun begins.

Shadows Weaving Through Infinity

In a land where shadows dance with glee,
They spin and twirl, not caring to flee.
Knocking over stars, they giggle and poke,
Whispering secrets, and sharing a joke.

The comets chime in with a twinkle and flair,
As aliens laugh, floating in midair.
Gravity trips them, they land with a splat,
Rolling in stardust, how silly is that?

Spaceships zoom by with a honking delight,
Passengers laughing at the funny sight.
With asteroids playing tag, round and round,
Who knew the cosmos could be so profound?

So let's join the fun, don a starry crown,
Where laughter and lightness will never let down.
In this zany universe, strange and bright,
The party continues all day and night!

A Passage to the Boundless

Through a tunnel of giggles, we jiggle and spin,
Where time gets so dizzy, we lose our own grin.
A parade of oddities, dressed in strange suits,
Laughing like children, all tickled by roots.

We glide past dimensions on inflatable clouds,
High-fiving old galaxies, shouting out loud!
Quarks in a conga, they shimmy and shake,
Turning physics to pudding, oh what a mistake!

In this realm of the wacky, the wild, and the weird,
We chase after comets, none truly revered.
Falling through portals while cracking a joke,
Who knew black holes had such a fun poke?

So come ride the wave of this cosmic charade,
Where laughter and lightyears can never quite fade.
With each silly step, let the journey unfold,
In this passage to boundless, together, we're bold!

Collisions with the Unfathomable

Bouncing around in a cosmic twirl,
We bump into nonsense and dizzying whirl.
Space-time is laughing, it's all gone awry,
As photons collide with cakes flying by.

With each silly crash, confetti explodes,
While planets roll over in animated todes.
Jupiter's juggling, oh what a delight,
Making us chuckle in the shadowy night.

Asteroid races make for the wildest chase,
Spinning and zipping through a soft, starry lace.
Gravity's teasing, it pulls and it tugs,
As quarks perform tangoes, swirled in snug hugs.

Each laugh echoes loud through the ether we roam,
Turning collisions to jokes, we feel right at home.
With giggles and wiggles, we share a grand tale,
As we dance with the unthinkable, forever set sail!

Surrendering to the Cosmic Flow

Float down the river of sheer silliness,
Where stars whistle tunes with delightful finesse.
The universe chuckles, a radiant mirth,
As planets play hopscotch, they're proving their worth.

We drift on a wave of whimsical light,
Embracing the chaos with all of our might.
The quasar's a clown, wearing socks out of phase,
It juggles black holes, putting us in a daze.

Supernova sprinkles with cosmic confetti,
Surrender to laughter, oh isn't it petty?
Galaxies winking, as we drift and we sway,
Sailing through space, on a bright starry day.

With stardust confessions in rippling streams,
We join in the giggles, fulfilling our dreams.
So let's ride the currents and dance in the glow,
Surrender to joy in this whimsical flow!

Ghosts of the Celestial Fringe

In the void where echoes play,
Ghosts of stars dance night and day.
Twinkling lights with a wink and grin,
Say, "Come join us, let the fun begin!"

Wormholes twist like spaghetti tight,
Aliens joke at the speed of light.
They drop their ice cream in a black hole,
And laugh about it—what a cosmic role!

Planets sneeze, they float away,
Jupiter just had a bad buffet.
Meteor showers like confetti falls,
Gravity's pulling on all our brawls!

So join the chase, don't hesitate,
In this realm of giggles, it's never too late.
Up in space, where fun takes flight,
Interstellar jokes are a sheer delight!

A Leap into the Starlit Unknown

Jumping through space, what a sight,
Stars are laughing, oh, what a flight!
Cosmic silliness in every beam,
Who knew the universe could be a dream?

Asteroids in tutus twirl and spin,
While comets giggle, "Come and join in!"
Galaxies swirling in a dance so strange,
Even dark matter takes time to change!

Space cows moo with a twinkling trill,
"Hey, Earthlings, come on, take a chill!"
Floating past, they munch on light,
Stellar snacks in the starry night.

So leap with glee into the void,
Where the absurd is never destroyed.
A snicker, a chuckle, in the vast unknown,
In this silly cosmos, you'll never alone!

The Dance of Distant Luminaries

Distant twinklers throw a bash,
With cosmic lights that flash and clash.
Stars in tutus spin and sway,
In the grand ballroom of the Milky Way!

"Step right up!" a supernova calls,
"Join the dance under celestial walls!"
Neutron stars join in with a beat,
Creating rhythms that can't be beat!

Black holes swing, a gravitational waltz,
With space dust drifting, no time for faults.
Jovial planets joke and sing,
Unicorns in space make everyone swing!

So spin with me in the starry space,
Where laughter echoes, and we embrace.
The dance of luminaries, what a sight,
In this cosmic party, we own the night!

Vanishing Point in the Cosmos

At the vanishing point, what do you see?
A raccoon astronaut sipping iced tea.
He grins and winks, says, "Join the fun!"
Under the laughter of the cosmic sun!

Planets hide behind cosmic trees,
Playing tag in a cosmic breeze.
Just don't be late, or you'll miss the gig,
An asteroid parade—now that's big!

Comets hoot, "We're on a roll!"
While spacebirds chirp, "Hey, feel the soul!"
Gravity's pulling, but we're floating free,
In this silly swirl of galactic jubilee.

So come and play, let's take a ride,
In the vanishing point where giggles abide.
Across the stars, in a comedic swirl,
The cosmos laughs, let's give it a whirl!

Resonance of the Cosmic Silence

Stars giggle, they wink, they tease,
In the void where no one sees.
Black holes doing silly dances,
Comets winking with wild glances.

Laughter echoing through the dark,
As light beams play a game of spark.
Gravity pulling all the pranks,
While planets roll in cosmic flanks.

Fragments of Reality's Fabric

Reality's threads are all askew,
A cosmic patchwork made for two.
Quasars strut in polka dots,
While pulsars play connect the dots.

In the fabric, I see a tear,
With aliens knitting without a care.
A universe with mismatched socks,
Stitching starlight on funny clocks.

The Cosmic Overlap

Galaxies stacked like pancake stacks,
With maple syrup from cosmic cracks.
Asteroids roll like bowling balls,
Knocking over space's silly stalls.

In this overlap, chaos reigns,
While martians play on silly trains.
Cosmic kids with bubblegum,
Pop the worlds—they're on the run!

Nightfall in Wonderland

When twilight tips and shadows play,
Giggles rise—it's time for fray.
Planets toss their hats in jest,
While the sun takes an evening rest.

In wonderland where odd things bloom,
Cats in hats all dance to tune.
Stars trade stories, laugh and gleam,
In this night, it's all a dream.

The Lure of the Unseen

In the dark where shadows play,
Jumping around, what a ballet!
Space squirrels dance in zany rows,
While cosmic dust gives all it knows.

A hitchhiking comet waves hello,
With a twinkle and a playful glow.
Aliens giggle, just out of sight,
Sharing tacos and silly flight.

Stars wear hats, oh what a sight!
Clumps of stardust take their flight.
While planets spin in jolly glee,
Wishing on wishes from the cosmic sea.

So come away, and join the jest,
In this realm where oddballs nest.
In the hush where laughter sings,
Unseen lures make the heart take wings.

Glimmers at the Cosmic Eventide

As the sun sinks low, a wink appears,
Jellybeans bounce, ignoring fears.
Galaxies giggle in spiraled cheer,
Tickling voids while we all jeer.

Nebulae sprout like wild daisies,
Inventing games that leave us crazy.
Warped-time kites flutter and soar,
Chasing echoes on a shop floor.

Each twinkling star a cheeky tease,
Playing tricks with the starlit breeze.
Cosmic laughter fills the air,
Winking at dreams beyond compare.

With cereal constellations at our feet,
The adventure's odd and oh-so-sweet.
So grab your ship and sail the rhyme,
In the glimmers of this spacey clime.

Whirlpools of Time's Fabric

Round and round the fabric spins,
Ants in space wear funny grins.
Tick-tock laughter echoes wide,
While time loops dance, oh what a ride!

Balloons of light float with glee,
Telling tales of galactic tea.
Riddles of time that whiz and zip,
Ask the moon for a fun-filled tip.

Gravity's tug gives a juicy sway,
Wormholes chuckle, join the play.
Like socks that vanish in the night,
Time's fabric sings with pure delight.

So if you find your day a bore,
Join the whirlpools, and laugh some more.
For in this dance, we spin and twirl,
In a universe, a wacky whirl.

Emissaries of the Dark Unknown

In shadows deep, the giggles reign,
With mischief hiding, just like rain.
Fluffly ghosts in top hats sway,
Leading lost socks in a wild ballet.

Beyond the veil, the humor breeds,
Unraveling space's funny needs.
Quasars hum a lullaby sweet,
As oddities create their feasts.

Jesters of black holes pull their pranks,
Filling voids with cosmic thanks.
Hiding beneath the astral glow,
With wink and nod, they steal the show.

So turn your gaze to the night sky,
And let laughter be your reply.
For in the unknown, where we roam,
The funniest tales find their home.

Voices from the Cosmic Abyss

In a black hole's hug, so very tight,
Stars are gossiping, what a sight!
They trade their tales, so wild and bold,
Whispers of mischief from days of old.

A comet sneezes, and off it goes,
In a supernova, a dance that glows!
Planets are laughing, they can't contain,
Space is a circus, in cosmic rain.

Aliens in pajamas, sipping their tea,
Pondering deep, 'What's the key?
To unlock the secret, the riddle supreme,
Or just to cook popcorn and dream a dream?'

So let's not take this galaxy too grim,
With twinkling lights and a sparkling whim.
The universe hums a silly tune,
Laughter erupts, beneath the moon!

The Last Glimpse of Daylight

As the sun dips low, it gives a wink,
Clouds puff up, in the colors we think.
The horizon giggles, a cheeky tease,
Is daylight playing hide-and-seek with ease?

Night owls in pajamas, ready to soar,
Counting the stars and searching for more.
The moon pulls a prank, it attaches a beam,
And tickles the daylight till it starts to scream!

Darkness arrives, dressed up in style,
With glittery stars from a cosmic pile.
They strut and they dance, with elegance rare,
Shining like diamonds in the cool night air.

So let's embrace the shadows' delight,
With goofy grins in the cool moonlight.
For each fleeting moment, let's cherish the play,
As night takes the stage, in a grand ballet!

Chasing Shadows Through Time

Shadows on the wall, they wiggle and sway,
Running from me like it's hide-and-seek day!
I trip over laughter, they giggle and zoom,
Into a dimension where fun starts to bloom.

Footsteps of time skip, hop, and twirl,
Chasing those shadows, oh what a whirl!
Past meets the future in a tangled dance,
All led by a cat with a curious glance.

Tick-tock is laughter, it spins in the air,
Time wears a hat with colors so rare.
We giggle together with each silly chase,
In the grand game of life, we find our place.

So let's bound through time, let our dreams interlace,
Dancing with shadows at a breakneck pace.
For in every tick, and every tock's chime,
There's a riddle of joy in chasing through time!

Dimensions Beyond the Fading Light

In a rabbit hole of giggles and glee,
Fading light wonders, 'What's next for me?'
A paperclip spaceship, ready to zoom,
Into dimensions where silliness blooms.

Bouncing through worlds, where unicorns shout,
With rainbow-colored socks, there's no doubt.
They throw a party, with cake and balloon,
And sing silly songs to the stars and the moon!

A dimension of dreams, where jellybeans sing,
Hopscotch with aliens? Oh, what a fling!
Invisible crayons paint nonsense galore,
While giggling shadows dance on the floor.

So take a leap, into worlds full of cheer,
Leave the worries behind, never fear!
For in each fading light, let hilarity ignite,
To reveal hidden gems of pure delight!

Tides of Dark Energy

In a space where time bends slow,
Tidal waves of light, oh no!
Stars swim by in comical glee,
Sipping tea from a cosmic sea.

Gravity pulls with a wobbly grin,
Spinning planets, let's begin!
Asteroids dodge like tiny bugs,
Dancing through those spacey hugs.

A black hole's belly begins to quake,
With a cosmic hiccup, make no mistake.
Out pops a quasar, what a sight,
Flashing jokes in the endless night.

So let's laugh as our fates unwind,
In this universe, hilarity's kind.
With every twist, a giggle awaits,
In the cosmos, let's celebrate our fates!

Flickers in the Eternal Night

In the dark where stars play hide and seek,
Lightbulbs flicker, they squeak and peek.
A comet zooms, but misses the fun,
A cosmic joke — not the chosen one.

Behind the void, a black cat strays,
Whiskers twitching in mysterious ways.
Ghostly satellites whisper and sigh,
Making sure they catch the high tide.

The Milky Way spills soda on its shirt,
Laughing as meteors flit and flirt.
Cosmic chaos in a wacky spree,
Even dark matter can't help but agree.

Galaxies giggle, what a delight!
In the endless dance of eternal night.
Every flicker tells a tale so bright,
In the universe where we find our light!

Curvature of Existence

Round and round like a donut's hole,
Curves in space tease the curious soul.
Twisting paths where we all take a spin,
Finding laughter in the chaos within.

Wormholes stretch like a cosmic grin,
Inviting all to hop right in.
Time ticks funny, it's never quite straight,
Snapping selfies with your future date!

Events collide, making quite a mess,
Puzzling together, we strive to guess.
Dimensions wobble, like jelly on toast,
In a universe where we all just coast.

So cheer for the bends, the loops, the twirls,
In this fabric of life where laughter unfurls.
With each quirky turn, let joy persist,
In the curvature where we can't resist!

The Dance of Celestial Bodies

When planets waltz with a cheeky flair,
Asteroids facepalm, floating in air.
Moons play tag with the glowing sun,
A cosmic party — oh boy, what fun!

Supernovae strut with glittering lights,
Spinning in circles, oh, what delights!
Stardust confetti rains down on the crowd,
Creating chuckles, exploding loud.

Galaxies twine in a pirouetting spree,
While comets juggle their tails with glee.
Quirky black holes pull drinks from afar,
Mixing cocktails with a cosmic star.

So let them dance, all day and night,
In this universe bursting with light.
For in the rhythm, joyfully we sway,
In the dance of bodies, let laughter play!

www.ingramcontent.com/pod-product-compliance
Lightning Source LLC
Chambersburg PA
CBHW071830160426
43209CB00003B/269